Treasury of Victorian Designs and Emblems

CD-ROM & Book

Palm & Fechteler

Dover Publications, Inc.
Mineola, New York

Bibliographical Note

Treasury of Victorian Designs and Emblems CD-ROM and Book, first published in 2006, includes a selection of 43 plates from a sample book of transfer ornaments for horse-drawn carriages, published by Palm & Fechteler, New York, in 1882.

Dover Electronic Clip Art®

International Standard Book Number: 0-486-99694-8

Manufactured in the United States of America
Dover Publications, Inc., 31 East 2nd Street, Mineola, N.Y. 11501

The CD-ROM on the inside back cover contains all of the images shown in the book. There is no installation necessary. Just insert the CD into your computer and call the images into your favorite software (refer to the documentation with your software for further instructions). Each image is saved in three different formats —300 dpi TIFF, high-resolution JPEG, and 72 dpi Internet-ready JPEG. The image can be used in a wide variety of word processing and graphics applications.

The "Images" folder on the CD contains a number of different folders. All of the TIFF images have been placed in one folder, as have all of the high-resolution JPEG and the 72-dpi JPEG. The images in each of these folders are identical except for file format. Every image has a file name that corresponds to the number printed with that image in the book.

For technical support, contact:
  Telephone: 1 (617) 249-0245
  Fax: 1 (617) 249-0245
  Email: dover@artimaging.com
  Internet: **http://www.dovertechsupport.com**
  The fastest way to receive technical support is via email or the Internet.

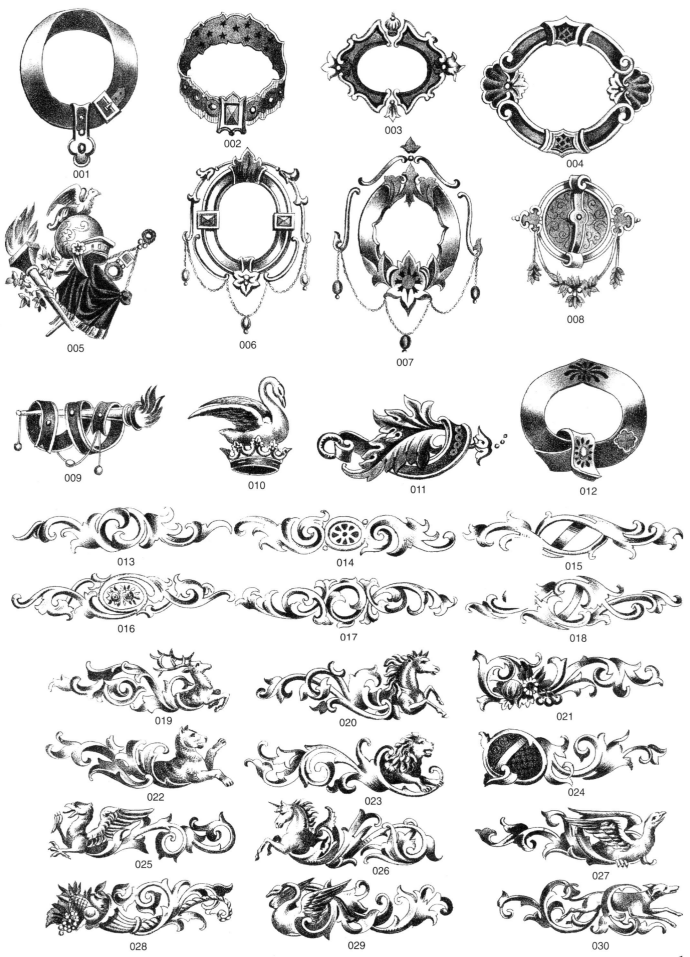

001

002

003

004

005

006

007

008

009

010

011

012

013

014

015

016

017

018

019

020

021

022

023

024

025

026

027

028

029

030

1

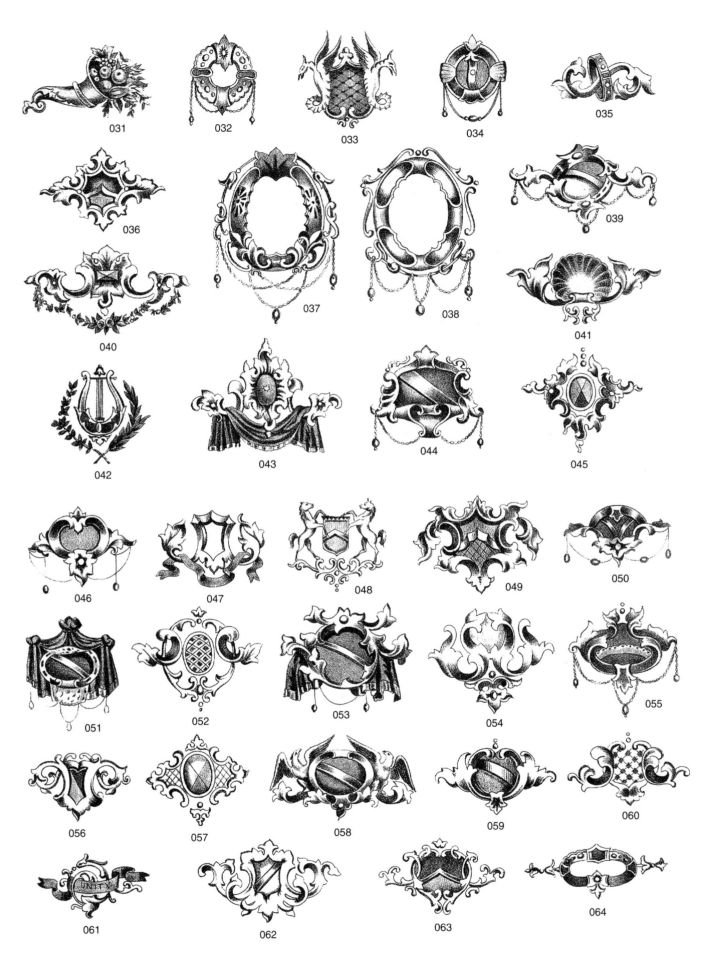

031 032 033 034 035
036 037 038 039
040 041
042 043 044 045
046 047 048 049 050
051 052 053 054 055
056 057 058 059 060
061 062 063 064

2

065   066   067   068   069
070   071   072   073
074   075   076   077   078
079   080   081   082   083
084   085   086   087   088   089
090   091   092   093   094
095   096   097   098   099
100   101   102   103   104

105   106   107   108   109

110   111   112   113   114

115   116   117   118   119

120   121   122   123   124

125   126   127   128   129   130   131

132   133   134   135   136   137   138

139   140   141   142   143   144   145

146   147   148   149   150   151   152

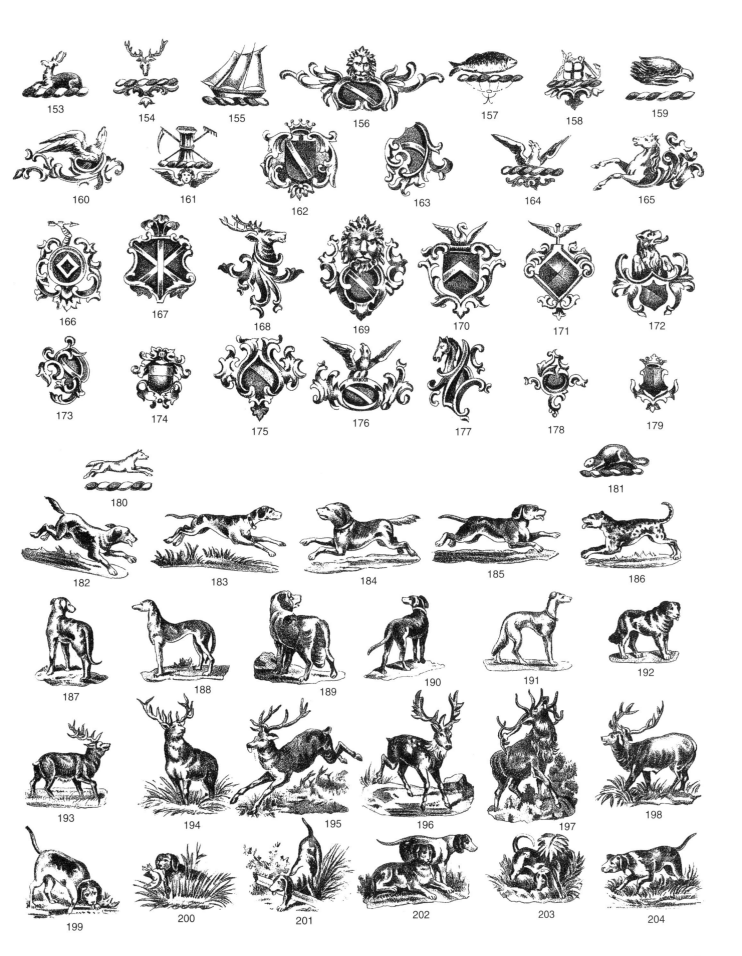

153 154 155 156 157 158 159

160 161 162 163 164 165

166 167 168 169 170 171 172

173 174 175 176 177 178 179

180 181

182 183 184 185 186

187 188 189 190 191 192

193 194 195 196 197 198

199 200 201 202 203 204

5

205   206   207   208   209   210

211   212   213   214   215

216   217   218   219   220   221

222   223   224   225   226   227   228

229   230   231   232   233   234   235

236   237   238   239   240   241

242   243   244   245   246   247

248   249   250   251   252   253

254   255   256   257

6

258

259

260

261

262

263

264

265

266

267

268

269

270

271

272

273

274

275

276

277

278

279

280

281

282

283

284

285

286

287

288

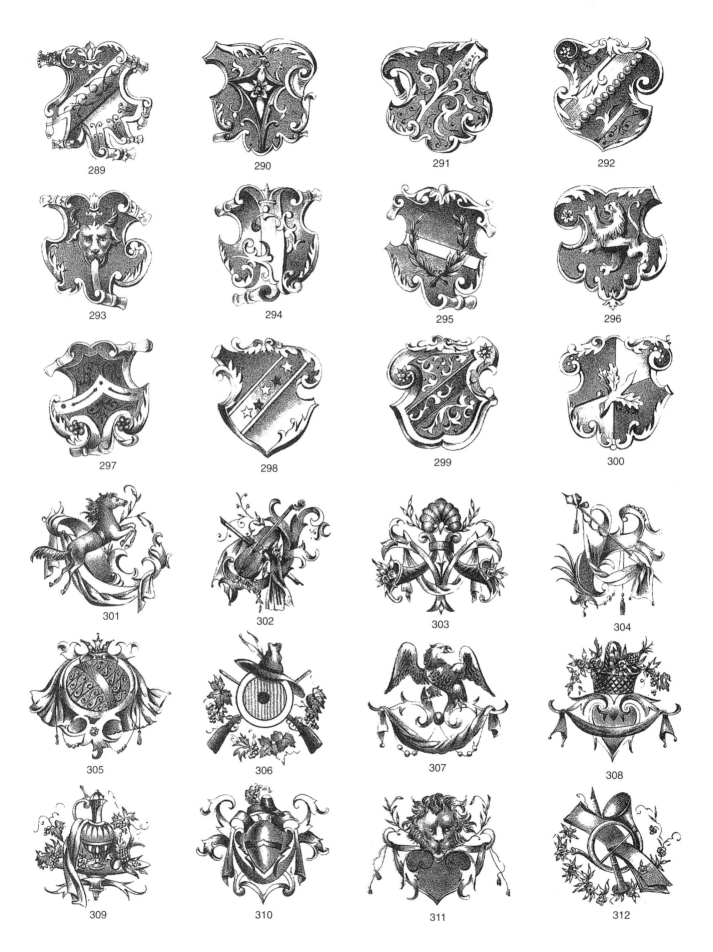

289 290 291 292
293 294 295 296
297 298 299 300
301 302 303 304
305 306 307 308
309 310 311 312

8

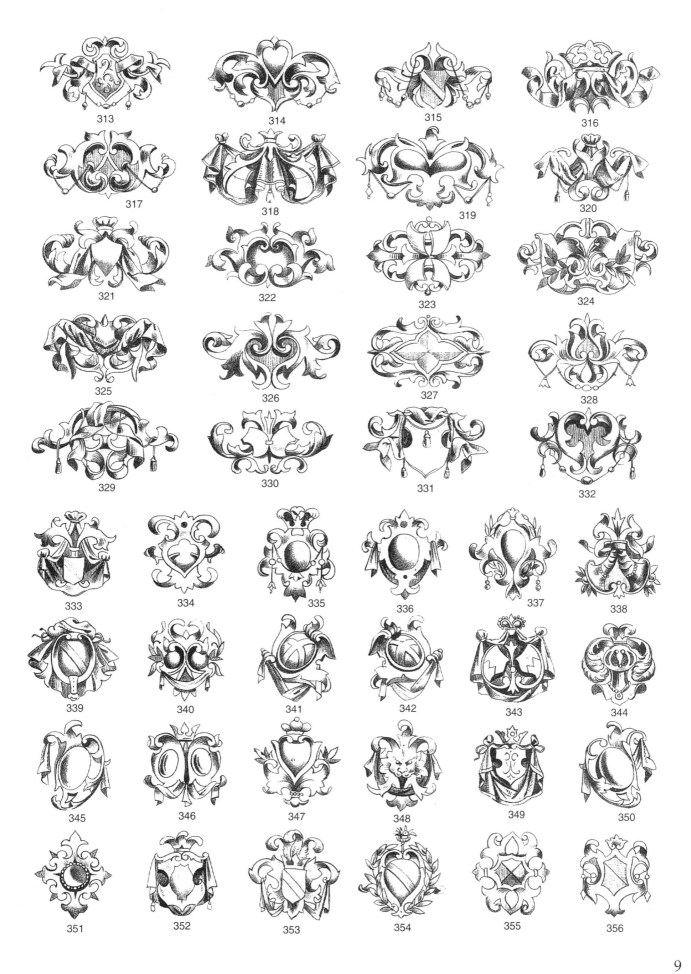

313 314 315 316

317 318 319 320

321 322 323 324

325 326 327 328

329 330 331 332

333 334 335 336 337 338

339 340 341 342 343 344

345 346 347 348 349 350

351 352 353 354 355 356

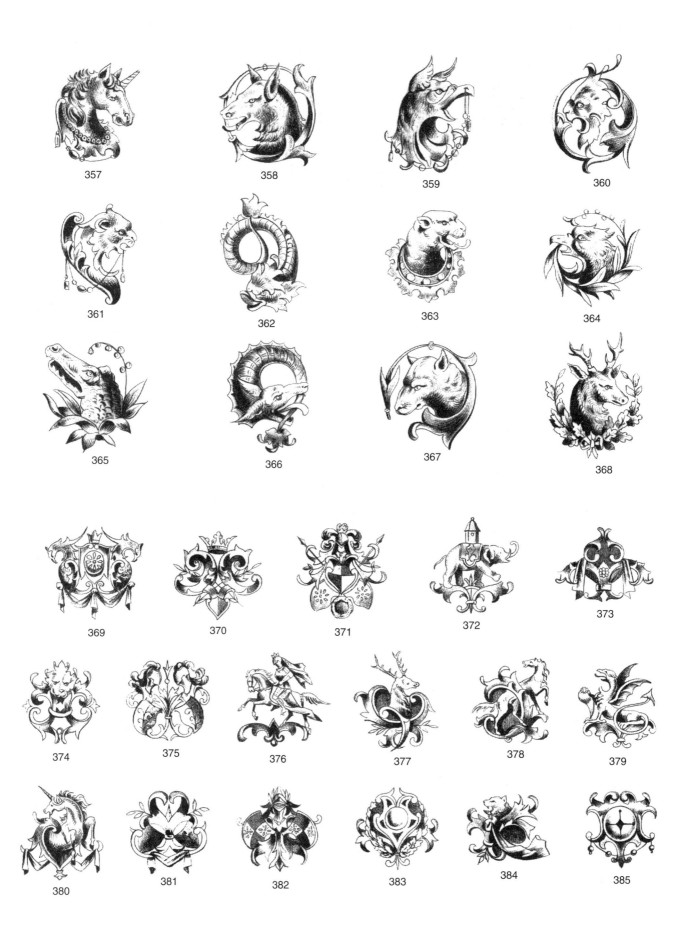

357

358

359

360

361

362

363

364

365

366

367

368

369

370

371

372

373

374

375

376

377

378

379

380

381

382

383

384

385

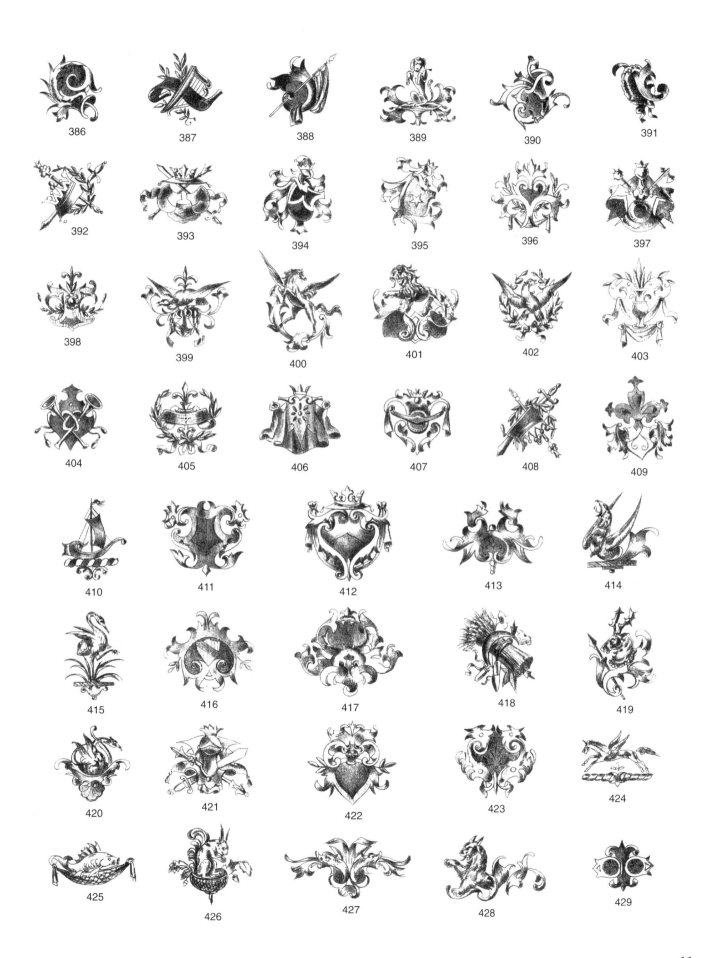

386 387 388 389 390 391

392 393 394 395 396 397

398 399 400 401 402 403

404 405 406 407 408 409

410 411 412 413 414

415 416 417 418 419

420 421 422 423 424

425 426 427 428 429

11

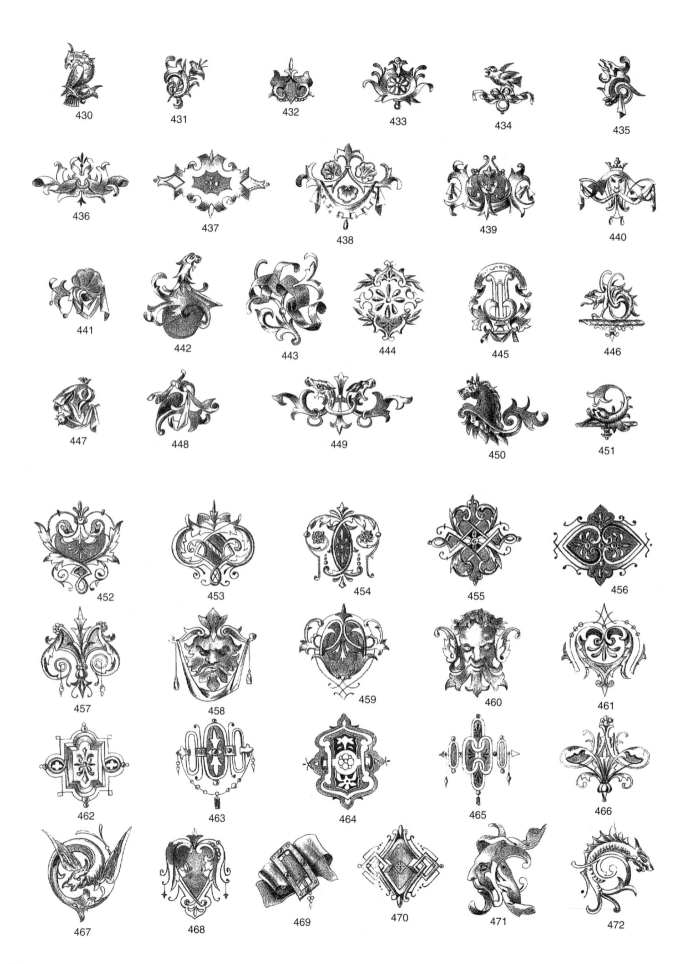

430

431

432

433

434

435

436

437

438

439

440

441

442

443

444

445

446

447

448

449

450

451

452

453

454

455

456

457

458

459

460

461

462

463

464

465

466

467

468

469

470

471

472

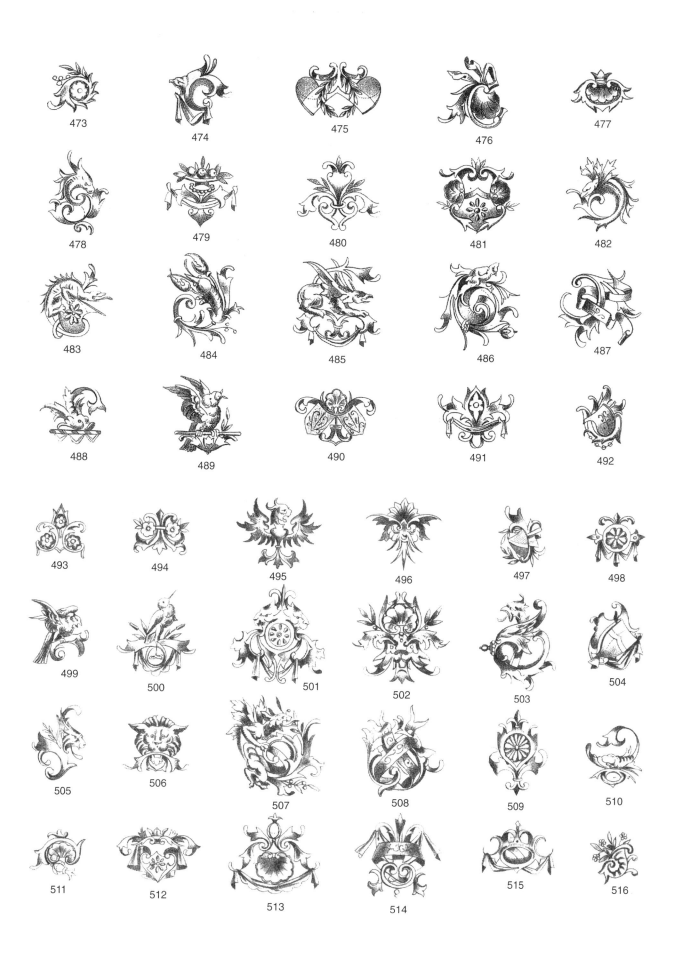

473
474
475
476
477
478
479
480
481
482
483
484
485
486
487
488
489
490
491
492
493
494
495
496
497
498
499
500
501
502
503
504
505
506
507
508
509
510
511
512
513
514
515
516

13

517

518

519

520

521

522

523

524

525

526

527

528

529

530

531

532

533

534

535

536

537

538

539

540

541

542

543

544

545

546

547

548

549

550

551

552

553

554

555

556

557

558

559

560

561

562

563

564

565

567

569

570

566

568

571

572

573

574

575

576

577

578

579

580

581

582

583

584

585

586

587

588

589

590

591

592

593

594

595

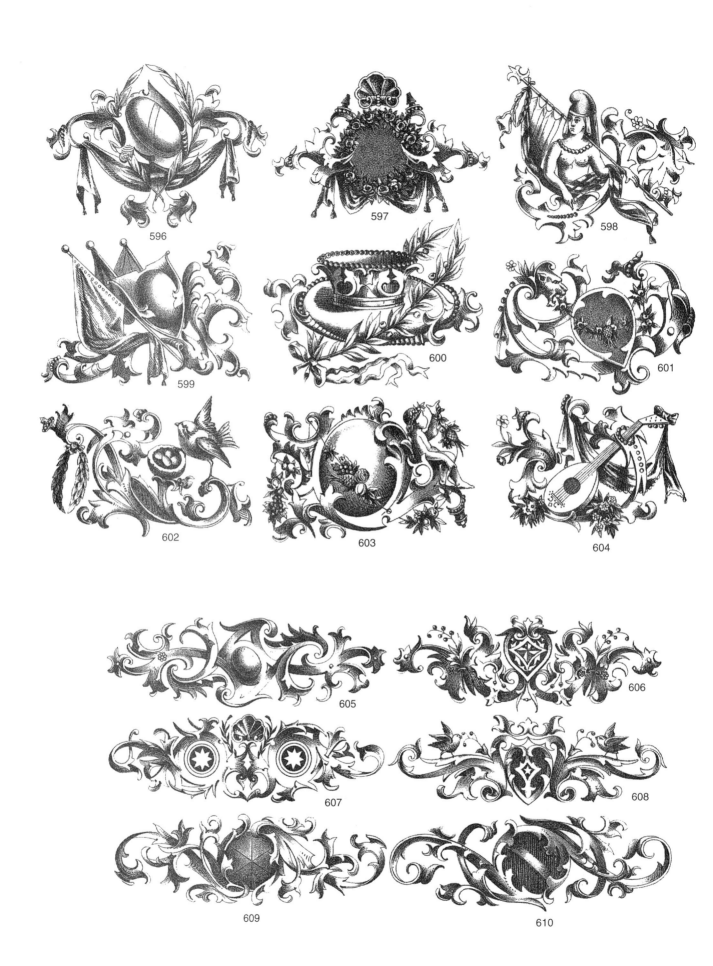

596

597

598

599

600

601

602

603

604

605

606

607

608

609

610

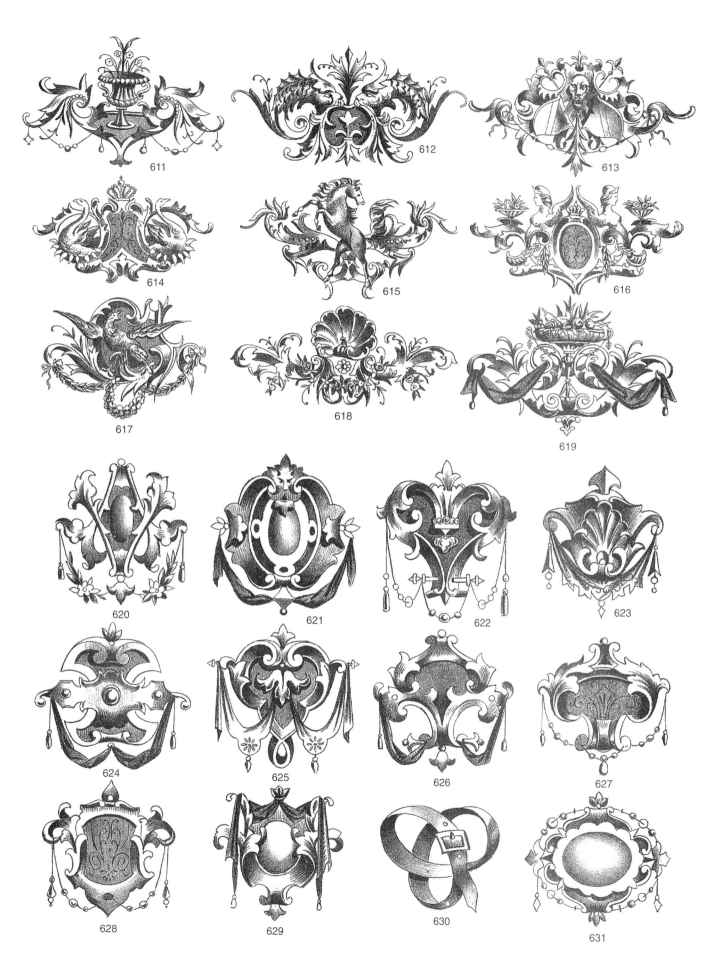

611   612   613
614   615   616
617   618   619
620   621   622   623
624   625   626   627
628   629   630   631

632

633

634

635

636

637

638

639

640

641

642

643

644

645

646

647

648

649

650

651

652

653

654

655

656

657

658

659

660

661

662

663

664

665

666

667

668

669

670

671

672

673

674

23

675

676

677

678

679

680

681

682

683

684

685

686

687

688

689

690

24

691

692

693

694

695

696

697

698

699

700

701

702

703

25

704   705   706   707   708
709   710   711   712   713
714   715   716   717   718
719   720   721   722   723
724   725   726   727   728
729   730   731   732   733
734   735   736   737   738
739   740   741   742   743

744 745 746 747 748 749

750 751 752 753 754 755

756 757 758 759 760 761

762 763 764 765 766 767 768

769 770 771

772 773 774 775 776

777 778 779 780 781

782 783 784 785 786

787 788 789

790 791 792 793

794

795

796

797

798

799

28

800

801

802

803

804

805

806

807

808

809

810

811

812

813

814

815

816

817

818

819

820

821

822

823

824

825

826

827

828

829

830

832

834

836

831

833

835

837

838

839

840

841

842

843

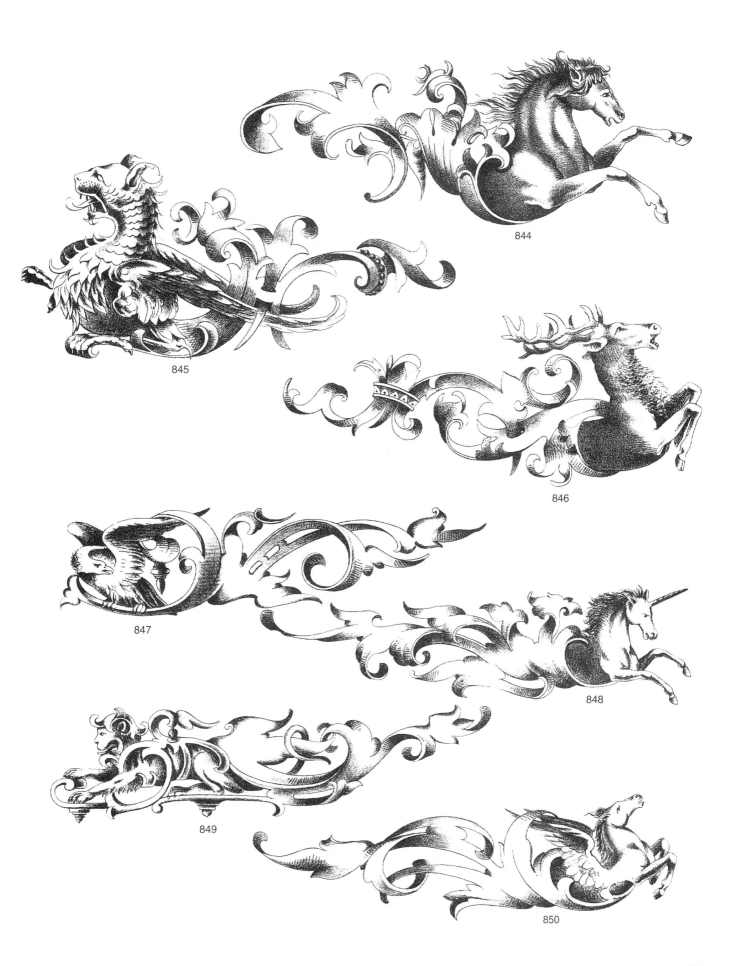

844

845

846

847

848

849

850

851

852

853

854

855

856

857

858

859

860

861

39

862

863

864

865

866

867

40

868

870

869

871

872

873

874

875

876

41

877

879

878

880

881

882

42

883

884

885

886

887

888

889

890

891

892

893